A BRAVE CRESCENDO

poems by

Abbie Copeland

Finishing Line Press
Georgetown, Kentucky

A BRAVE CRESCENDO

ACKNOWLEDGMENTS

"Beauty" was first published in *Foliate Oak Literary Magazine* in December
2014.

Publisher: Leah Maines
Editor: Christen Kincaid
Cover Art: Alex Stuart https://unsplash.com/photos/MVQfvQl_Jg8
Author Photo: The More We See, www.themorewesee.com
Cover Design: Abbie Copeland

Printed in the USA on acid-free paper.
Order online: www.finishinglinepress.com
           also available on amazon.com

Author inquiries and mail orders:
Finishing Line Press
P. O. Box 1626
Georgetown, Kentucky 40324
U. S. A.

Table of Contents

For Steve & Talula—
You give me strength and love.
Always and forever.

antibodies

there's a time to resist
but this is not one of those times.

and I bet she's still wishing for it

although she watched my veins
drained and emptied and
pulled out of my arms.

they take these antibodies and
turn them into numbers on a chart,
and say

you should really
not be here, standing.
you should really not be.

I'm fighting it like a bad flu
but you are still going back
to pour them more
and the reasons:

1. because your body moves like cooled liquid butter
2. you'd like to numb a portion of your body, in this case, the finger tips
3. the pain explained and the de–

pressing on
with tiny red circles
with writing too small to read.

and yet you are still on the
anti-thyroid peroxidase antibodies
conversation

and mine were elevated
but they were mine.
let them be.

a brave crescendo

like a shell I cup my hand over my ear
and I can hear the songs of my childhood,

moans of a man with a high pitch voice
and he's talking about love.

but I'm fixated on what the word is
for a man's genitalia.

the bathtub is warm and full of oatmeal,
and I call it a "saw."

I say it out loud. He has a *saw*.

but my senses are muddled and I know
I'm hurling words at the wall,

because I lacked the words to describe
and to react to what I saw.

Like a chainsaw? my mother asks.
No.
Like a wood cutting saw? my mother asks.
No.

But I don't actually call her *mother*
and she actually knows what I mean.

It's not, she says. *It's not called a saw.*
and my little naked body is stinging

from the oatmeal bath as I pick at
red bumps, so many little red bumps

and try to hear an ocean's swell
in my hand shell from an ocean
1000 miles away.

fix

she's more delicate
than I thought.

but that's the way
it's supposed to be,

>   her
>   outside, free.

I've mustered up the courage
to lock myself
in the bathroom

to let her rage,
to let me rage,
to let us fall into place.

>   she's all
>   squinty eyed *I love you's*

and my waist-less wasted
but no, I would do it again.

>   *but it's harder when you're older*
>   *and the damage is done.*

I'm telling her stories about
vampire slayers and zombies
and bumps in the night.

brave bits
when she's singing
songs in the dark

brave Miss
when she's standing alone
in a crowd.

trained

conditioned
in what was
a pernicious
obedience school.

the instructor said *obey*
while my body buzzed electric,
and my heart pulled toward
a squirrel or raw meat.

I'm a bad girl
who's suffering from
some sort of
shock collar syndrome.

days end

at night,
I rubbed your back

counted your freckles
and birth marks, dark circles

and abysmal shapes
melting into the folds.

I clung to the chestnut
of your hair

while you folded towels
like bread dough

and sang tiny lullabies
to sandwiches.

amputee

we used to cut people
off like limbs,
you and I.

yes you,
a Jersey boy with not one,
nor two,
but three terrible lessons
under his belt
muttering prayers to St. Matthew

God and Mary with you

and I,
a boorish belle,
a sweet tea hope.
you said
you could smell the violence
on me.

we purposely knotted our limbs
double, triple
and with precise cuts
I'll sever you

and yet I know
I still won't be
quite through
with you.

dissect

sometimes it's not about
whom you lose,
but what you lose.

and you learned to take
great care
of you and yours.

you learned to write
with a full plate

and find yourself
gently folded
into two,

head to knees,
breathing shallow.

it's been 7 years
since you lost your
mother

and you are reminded
that the whole unit
is devastated

and it feels unnatural
because it is.

environment

I find too much
of her in me

(and me in her)

but we are one of the same.

I had no mother
like me

and she had no mother
like mine.

she begs
for my soft belly

and I tuck
pieces of hair

behind her
gold earlobe.

anti-depressed

I lack the words
to measure pain
and admit

that in the
way back when,
I learned

   to like/accept

the abuse.

and I'm still finding
visceral reactions
to outside stimuli

and it's the only way I can
learn to be a little
kinder to my
self.

going slow, going deep,
even if the
instructor is yelling

   this is an *open* eye meditation.

dirty girl

I'm blushing because I know
you are thinking of something
singular and sweet.

and you've poured it all over me
but my body can't handle
those type of truths.

I've progressed to progressive
a kinky sweet Southern thing,

and sometimes I'm blonde
and other times I'm multi.

I can make distance come to me
by moving my hands over my
hip bones and I remember when

I had no hip bones, and I had no
collar bones and I cupped my breasts
at night for comfort

whispering that they were *mine*
and wishing one day that they would be.

the end of a (friend)ship

I am sitting,
sailing,

in a well thought out
              circle,
                cycle,

perhaps a deep incline.

and the loss is profound
and worth ruminating over.

I watched sentiment
spray from your mouth
like cheap window cleaner.

and missing an oar,
missing two,

missing the distance
from where we never were.

sisters

as children we played
because we only had

our necessary type of
existence. and still

we used to be sweet,
crabgrass and dandelion crowns,
waiting for the cicada song.

the jungle gym will rust
and be disassembled

and we will try to recall
how we were left to train
rolly pollies in the palms
of our hands.

mrs/maternal

the playground is full
of daft little curls—

ringlets around mommy's finger,
breast-feds and organic grown.

> *she's really a bright one.*
> *brighter than a dying star.*

I'd rather be curled up with mine
fiddling with spoons & pots,

squeaky echoes,
spell checked messages,
abbreviated annoyances.

> *I have a purpose.*
> *My purpose is this.*

we are betrayed by this old folklore
and the mundane questions
always have the same answer.

Let her be.
Let her grow.
Let her strive.

> *we are built to love and create*
> *those who will watch us die.*

crush

she was a tall drink of tea,
too hot to steep,
and radiated dial tones.

I can still picture her
pressing down
on someone else,

bodies like naked trees
but the burn of the sun
will betray her.

flesh folds

a naughty reminder
there are still ashes
in old purses
and I can remember
the way meat tastes.

with her

eyeing the same sex
is an investigative
practice

so we made love
with our facial
expressions.

she told me about
throwing up on Dylan
and grabbing Bowie's
thigh.

I found courage
in disinterest,

sipping blood orange
margaritas

watching heat rise
from her finger tips.

grown

now I find you've grown
manish and towering over
ancient things

and still I found
solace in the stalking.

watching your picture
morph like
a repeated visit
to a garden I didn't
tend to.

you found structure in your growth
and deep moments of
depravity.

I realize your intentions with women
a stem of a root
of me.

and you said

> *Oh, I'm a fuckboy.*
> *I'm a fuck*
> *boy.*

still reminiscent of
a childhood you had not yet
crawled out of.

the house is for sale

for sale:
yellow wainscoting in the bathroom,
peeling cherry cabinets in the kitchen,
rust spots on the back porch,
dead hostas and pansies,
paint bleached by the sun,
clutter counters covered
with unused appliances
and bottles of
cooking oil and lotion,
a living room with pictureless walls
taupe trim and a torn up couch.
warped floors,
wall to wall carpet,
dusty closet space and
a half bath filled with
half burned cigarette butts.

  I used to watch patches of grass
  die under the kiddie pool.

  I used to watch the dog dig holes
  under the rotted fence.

  I used to hide behind the shed
  and drink vodka from a water bottle.

  I did my time,
  I did my time.
  and the price still isn't right.

to live by default

there's that
overpopulation problem
anyway.

and there's blanks
or ropes and cords
or belts too short

and pills you shouldn't
mix but can

(who knew)

and I can change my mind
but decide to keep
all of the above
anyway,
even if it's hard and
heavy and unseen.

and no matter how
hard I try to peel
off these layers

the world, you know,
has many, many layers

it still feels like
I just might sink

because the world is
mostly water
and so are we

and apparently I
you
we are all
made of stars

or the same stuff as stars
and my heart wants to
believe that.

because the thought
of being a star

or rather made of stars

feels tender and sweet
and I haven't felt that way
in a long time.

nouveau

side splitting with erotic undertones
and all I know is you are finding a way
to make sense of unfortunate circumstances

like line breaks in news casts,
harsh rhetoric from old white men
who talk about wombs like

      they remember it.

here,
still here,
warm and still.

but watching them fight in wood panel is more like
sliding a wad of cotton in a dry area

      which is not up
      for discussion today.

you make an off the cuff remark
of how

      they're just trying to get back in there.
      always trying to figure out a way back in.

it's the punch line
that gets me
but the truth,
it still hurts.

marathon

my legs are so heavy
and I imagine this is what
polio feels like.

> *and that's a terrible thing to say*
> *because I'm not diseased.*
> *I'm just running.*

or slogging
because that's a better term
for mile 24.

but everyone's suffering,
everyone's in their own pain.
their faces contorted
and twisted,

squeezing water into their mouth,
silent on a highway,
scattered like dots on asphalt.

I know what it's like to be in pain,
surrounded and alone,

and suddenly I'm revived
knowing I've done this before.

beauty

she was beautiful
because she decided to be
open.

soft belly massage,
gaping tongue,
ravaging herself like
pink begonias.

that dress that hung
just barely off the hanger
slipped on smooth and
fitted,

she decided to let go,
bushy eyebrows and all
dimpled and pimpled,
protruding collar bones.

it was a good day
because she remembered
to water everything
and let filtered light in
at the right angle.

ADDITIONAL ACKNOWLEDGEMENTS

To Leah, Christen, Ryan and everyone at Finishing Line Press—Thank you for your support and for believing in *A Brave Crescendo*. I am forever grateful my words found a home with FLP.

To my dearest Donna and Helen, the first readers of *A Brave Crescendo*—Thank you for believing in me and in this book and most importantly, for your love. And to Karen, my ride or die—Thank you for 16 years of friendship, love, and support. Not by blood, but by love, you are my family.

Thank you to Dina for your ears and eyes, your inspiration and your friendship. I admire you as a writer, friend, mother, and woman.

To all my friends—Thank you for inspiring me and filling me with love. Without your support, I would not be able to do what I do. You are forever in my heart.

To my daughter, Talula—My heart, my greatest cheerleader, my muse. You continue to amaze me. You've made me a stronger woman, and I am so proud to be your mom.

And a very special thank you to my husband, Steve—For the emotional labor it took to read this book and to support me for all that has happened to write this book. You are my rock and my green eyes. Thank you for your love, support, and companionship.

Abbie Copeland is a writer and editor. Her work has appeared in a variety of online and print publications including *Open Minds Quarterly, The Pedestal Magazine, Bacopa Literary Review, Vestal Review, Foliate Oak Literary Magazine*, and others. Her flash fiction story, "Bed Bugs" was nominated for a Pushcart Prize and received a Write Well Award by the Silver Pen Association in 2015. Abbie is also the founder and editor-in-chief of *Dying Dahlia Review*, an online literary journal featuring poetry, flash fiction and art by women writers and artists. She graduated from Kean University with a B.A. in English. She currently resides in Lambertville, New Jersey with her husband and daughter.

CPSIA information can be obtained
at www.ICGtesting.com
Printed in the USA
BVHW032015200519
548769BV00019B/156/P